AFFIRMING

Giles

CHRISTIANITY AND VIOLENCE:

GIRARD, NIETZSCHE, ANSELM AND TUTU

Series Editor: Mark D. Chapman

DARTON·LONGMAN+TODD

First published in 2001 by
Darton, Longman and Todd Ltd
1 Spencer Court
140–142 Wandsworth High Street
London SW18 4JJ

in association with

Affirming Catholicism
St Luke's Centre
90 Central Street
London EC1V 8AQ

ISBN 0–232–52416–5

The views expressed in this book are those of the author
and do not necessarily reflect any policy of
Affirming Catholicism.

Unless otherwise stated, the Scriptural quotations
in this booklet are taken from the Revised Standard Version
© Division of Christian Education of the National Council
of the Churches of Christ, 1971.

Designed by Sandie Boccacci
Phototypeset in 10/13pt Times by Intype London Ltd
Printed and bound in Great Britain by
Page Bros, Norwich, Norfolk

Affirming Catholicism

Affirming Catholicism is a movement (not an ecclesiastical party) which exists to do two things. We affirm our confidence in our Anglican heritage; and we seek to renew and promote the Catholic tradition within it. Our aim is to explore, explain and share with others both inside and outside the Church a lively, intelligent and inclusive Catholic faith. In the words of our Trust Deed:

> It is the conviction of many that a respect for scholarship and free enquiry has been characteristic of the Church of England and of the Churches of the wider Anglican Communion from earliest times, and is fully consistent with the status of those Churches as part of the Holy Catholic Church. It is desired to establish a charitable educational foundation which will be true both to those characteristics and to the Catholic tradition within Anglicanism...The object of the foundation shall be the advancement of education in the doctrines and the historical development of the Church of England and the Churches of the wider Anglican Communion, as held by those standing within the Catholic tradition.

Our Publications

These are offered as one means of presenting Anglican Catholic teaching and practice in as clear and accessible a form as possible. Some cover traditional doctrinal and liturgical themes: others attempt to present a well-argued

Catholic viewpoint on issues of debate currently facing the Church. There is a list of our series of booklets on page v.

To order these publications individually or on subscription, or for further information about the aims and activities of Affirming Catholicism, write to:

The Secretary
Affirming Catholicism
St Luke's Centre
90 Central Street
London EC1V 8AQ

Tel: 020 7253 1138
Fax: 020 7253 1139

Books in the Affirming Catholicism series

Contents

The mechanism of reciprocal violence can be described as a vicious circle. Once a community enters the circle, it is unable to extricate itself. We can define this circle in terms of vengeance and reprisals, and we can offer diverse psychological descriptions of these reactions. As long as a working capital of accumulated hatred and suspicion exists at the centre of a community, it will continue to increase no matter what men do. Each person prepares himself for the probable aggression of his neighbours and interprets his neighbours' preparations as confirmation of the latter's aggressiveness. In more general terms, the mimetic character of violence is so intense that once installed in a community, it cannot burn itself out.

To escape from the circle it is first necessary to remove from the scene all those forms of violence that tend to be self-propagating and to spawn new, imitative forms.

René Girard, *Violence and the Sacred*

Introduction:
Why Violence? Why Girard?

The World Council of Churches plans to designate
the first decade of the twenty-first century as one
in which the Churches confront issues of violence.
Dr Konrad Raiser, the general secretary of the
WCC, has spoken of the need to 'enter into a self-
critical assessment of those theological, ecclesiastical or cultural traditions which tend to justify
violence in the name of defending order and
enforcing obedience'. This booklet is a response to
that invitation.

Of the many and varied attacks upon religious
belief rehearsed over the centuries, the one which
manages to touch a nerve like no other is the accu-
sation that religion breeds violence. Laying side by
side Jesus' unambiguous message that we love one
another with the history of violence with which
the Christian faith has been associated is the most
painful of juxtapositions. *Christianity and Violence*
seeks to interrogate this contradiction and does so
by taking seriously claims that this history of violence results not just from sectarianism, or from
the actions of wicked individuals who have played
prominent roles in the Church's history, but has
been generated deep down within Christian
theology. It will consider the idea that the dispo-

sition towards violence is rooted in some of the most fundamental conceptions of the Christian faith.

Arguably, the thinker who in recent times has done most to examine the nature of this 'genetic flaw' is the French Roman Catholic anthropologist René Girard. Girard's thought is not as widely known as it ought to be and though this short booklet cannot seek to do justice to the richness of his thinking, it may spur readers on to look more closely at his work for themselves. Girard's thought, his supporters claim, provides a way of re-working some of the major themes of Christian theology which is, at the same time, both revolutionary and wholly faithful to the theology of Jesus. A crucial part of Jesus' theology, Girard claims, was to reveal this hidden disposition towards violence – 'I will utter what has been hidden since the foundation of the world' as Jesus puts it in Matthew 13:35, and from which Girard takes the title of his main book on the subject. A good deal of subsequent theology has, according to Girard, betrayed Jesus' attempt to root out the tendency of religion towards violence and has re-invented a theology, particularly on the matter of the significance of his death, which is in direct opposition to his teachings. If Girard is correct, this is a matter of utmost importance to all Christians. What's at stake here is nothing less than the very nature of God's will for the world. .

1. Christianity: A Religion of Violence?

'You read the Bible, Bret?' Bret doesn't know what to say. He is terrified, convulsed with a spasm caused by the bullet in his shoulder. His soon-to-be assassin menaces over him with the gun now pointing at his head. 'There's a passage I got memorized, seems appropriate for this situation: Ezekiel 25:17. The path of the righteous man is beset on all sides by the iniquities of the selfish and the tyranny of evil men. Blessed is he who, in the name of charity and good will, shepherds the weak through the valley of darkness, for he is truly his brother's keeper and the finder of lost children. And I will strike down upon thee with great vengeance and furious anger those who attempt to poison and destroy my brothers. And you will know my name is the Lord when I lay my vengeance upon you.' Jules empties the gun in Bret's face. The directions in the screen play state: 'When they are finished, the bullet-ridden carcass just sits there for a moment, then topples over.'[1]

One of Quentin Tarantino's many talents as a film-writer is to have an ear for the authentic voice of violence. His appropriation of mock Biblical language in this scene from the cult movie *Pulp Fiction*, however over-stylised, reminds us of the presence of that voice throughout the scriptures. In fact, only the last line of Jules' speech is to be found in Ezekiel 25:17 – 'I will carry out great vengeance on them and punish them in my wrath. Then they will know that I am the LORD, when I take vengeance on them' – but who can deny that Jules' pulp theology sounds distinctively Biblical. 'I never really questioned what it meant,' Jules admits towards the end of the film, 'I just thought it was a cold-blooded thing to say.' Jules simply (mis)quotes Ezekiel to terrify his victims. And it works. For the truth is that the Bible is full of violence and the language of violence.

These 'texts of terror' (a phrase coined by Phyllis Trible to refer to those passages of the Bible which have been used to sanction violence against women) are, in fact, more common than we might like or are often prepared to admit. Look at Deuteronomy 17:14ff. Think of the violence of the Levitical prohibitions. Think of the violence of the Psalms. Let one example of these stand for many. Consider a passage from Psalm 58:

> O God, break the teeth in their mouths;
>> tear out the fangs of the young lions, O Lord!
> Let them vanish like water that runs away;
>> like grass let them be trodden down and wither.
> Let them be like the snail that dissolves into slime;
>> like the untimely birth that never sees the sun.

Sooner than your pots can feel the heat of thorns,
    whether green or ablaze, may he sweep them
    away!
The righteous will rejoice when they see ven-
    geance done;
they will bathe their feet in the blood of the
    wicked.

                         (NRSV Psalm 58:7–11)

It won't do simply to bracket out these passages as
though they didn't exist.[2] Still less is it acceptable
to dismiss the Old Testament as presenting us with
a 'violent' and 'vengeful' God in contrast to the
'peace-loving' God of the New Testament. This, of
course, is Marcionism, the heretical Gnostic doctrine that rejects the Old Testament 'creator God'
as evil and as being wholly superseded by the 'mer-
ciful God' of the New Testament. Some of the more
naive treatments of the law/grace distinction come
very close to repeating this heresy. In its ugliest
form, it becomes the basis for the sort of theology
employed by Nazi 'Christians' keen to eradicate
the Jewishness of the Bible.

    Of course, mentioning the Nazis in the context
of a discussion of Christianity and violence reminds
us of the extent to which the Christian tradition
has been responsible for the invention and development of that most pernicious of violent
ideologies: anti-Semitism. Coming from a Jewish
background myself, more than once I have felt
that in becoming a Christian I have sided with the

persecutors against the persecuted. It is the most tragic of ironies that the murder of one Jew should have proved the pretext for the murder of so many others. But it is not just Jews that have lost their lives 'in remembrance of me'. As I walk to work every day I pass the spot in Oxford outside Balliol College where the Protestant Bishops Cranmer, Ridley and Latimer were, like countless others, burned to death by fellow Christians whose theological perspective they did not share. These are instances of violence that impact upon my imagination daily and reflect my personal circumstances. You don't have to live in Belfast or Kosovo or Jerusalem to live in a place scarred by Christian violence.

I was struck by a story I came across recently about a sailor who finds himself washed up on an unknown shore after a shipwreck. Lost, he looks around for familiar landmarks or indications of what country he is in. Seeing a dead man hanging from a gibbet, the sailor immediately praises God that he has found himself in a Christian country![3] It's not just that Christianity has a history of inquisitions, persecutions, executions and crusades – to leave the analysis there would be to invite the superficial explanation that violence done in the name of God is done by wicked individuals who have misunderstood Christianity. No, if we are going to engage with 'Christian violence' fully we have to be prepared to recognise it at the very heart of Christian belief.

For Girard, the root of religious violence is to be found in the workings of what he calls the 'sacrificial mechanism'. What he purports to explain is how a certain conception of religion is founded upon violence and that, however buried and obscured from view, this founding violence will continue to manifest itself unless it is exposed and set right. Hence: 'I will utter what has been hidden since the foundation of the world'. But before we come on to Girard who is himself a Christian and so believes 'religion' can be redeemed from its capacity for violence, let us make space for a much more hostile voice. For, as we shall see, it is one of the gains of Girard's position that he offers a way of responding to perhaps the most vociferous attack on Christianity ever conducted. Before we try and unscramble the problem let us make things as difficult as possible for ourselves. Let us turn to that great genius of anti-Christianity, Friedrich Nietzsche.

2. Nietzsche's Charge of *Ressentiment*

Here, in brief, is Nietzsche's alternative myth of salvation history. In the beginning all was well. People lived freely and happily – and God was an expression of the good conscience of those who believed in God. Belief in God was, above all, an extension of human self-affirmation. This, Nietzsche believes, represents a healthy spirituality. The 'fall' begins with the capture and enslavement of the people of God. For once in captivity the link is broken between God and human flourishing. How could a God who was the expression of a nation's self-confidence survive the deportation of his people? God had to be re-imagined. Re-imagined, that is, from the perspective of the victim.

Nietzsche's fundamental insight is that victims come to poison healthy spirituality. How so? First of all because persecution incubates and intensifies feeling of hatred towards oppressors. Captivity, Nietzsche insists, is a breeding ground for fantasies of violence. 'Out of this powerlessness their hate swells into something huge and uncanny,' as he puts it. Consider Psalm 137. It begins with a lament about the circumstances of captivity, 'By the rivers of Babylon we sat down and wept', and concludes with an encouragement of the more terrible ferocity: 'happy is he who repays you for what you have done to us – he who seizes your infants and dashes them against the rocks' (NIV). Christianity is, for Nietzsche, fundamentally the religion of the oppressed, the religion of slaves and, as such, it is impregnated with the desire for revenge or *ressentiment*. Unable to discharge their desire for retribution upon their captors in acts of physical violence, the oppressed sublimate retributive instincts into their conception of God. God becomes a vehicle for imagined revenge upon the oppressors. God becomes a God of vengeance. One of the most obvious expressions of this desire for vengeance is to be found in the rhetoric of divine punishment. Nietzsche points to Tertullian's description of seeing one's enemies in hell:

> What ample breadth of sights there will be then! At which shall one gaze in wonder? At which shall I laugh? At which rejoice? At which exult, when I see so many kings who were proclaimed to have been taken up into heaven, groaning in the deepest darkness? And when I see those governors, persecutors of the Lord's name, melting in the flames more savage than those with which they insolently raged against Christians! . . . I believe that they [these sights] are more pleasing than the circus or both of the enclosures, or than any racetrack.[4]

For Tertullian the sight of burning people is a pleasurable spectacle that makes heaven all the more worthwhile. Nietzsche concludes that above the gate of paradise should be written: 'Eternal hate created me as well'. For Nietzsche, it is the terrible genius of Christianity to proclaim and celebrate as love that which is basically the product of hate.

Nietzsche's story is not just about the consequences of the exile. He is seeking to bring out the logic whereby victims of bullying turn into bullies themselves, of how the abused can become the abusers. Christianity, with all its compassion for the victim, has a dangerous blind spot here. And Nietzsche seeks to reveal in the hurt and pain of the victim the seeds of new forms of hurt and pain which victims visit both upon others and revisit upon themselves.

One of Nietzsche's most penetrating suggestions is that the hate which is produced by oppression comes to have a life of its own that is independent of the circumstances of its birth. Partly because it has been so successfully incorporated into the theological imagination and partly because it is a temptation to which human beings readily succumb, *ressentiment* is able to mutate so as to adapt to different circumstances. Consequently *ressentiment* has many manifestations and goes by a number of different disguises. One such mutation is that which commonly occurs in periods of peace and prosperity. Hatred requires something to hate if it is to survive. But if we have no enemies who is there left to hate? What happens when Christianity becomes the religion not of the downtrodden but that of the establishment, that of the comfortable bourgeoisie? Nietzsche's response is that without an enemy to hate we come to hate ourselves.

> Lacking external enemies and obstacles, and forced into the oppressive narrowness of conformity and custom, man impatiently ripped himself apart, persecuted himself, gnawed at himself, gave himself no peace and abused himself, this animal who battered himself raw on the bars of his cage and who is supposed to be 'tamed'; man full of emptiness and torn apart for homesickness for the desert, has to create from within himself an adventure, a torture-chamber, an unsafe and hazardous wilderness – this fool, this prisoner consumed with longing and despair, became the inventor of the 'bad conscience'. With it, however, the worst and most insidious illness was introduced, one from which man has not yet recovered, man's sickness of man, of himself.[5]

Having demonstrated the ways in which *ressentiment* takes root, Nietzsche proceeds to argue that far from being rejected by the religious establishment, *ressentiment* is claimed by the Church as a source of power. In order to cement their control over this source of power the 'priests' develop a theology of guilt, of sin, and eventually of forgiveness, which allows them to be the mediators of a complex mechanism of punishment and reward.

The prophets, for instance, respond to the experience of exile by proclaiming that the suffering experienced by Israel represents a punishment for past sins. The tremendous power of *ressentiment* is harnessed by ancient religious spin-doctors (just as Eliphaz, Bildad and Zophar seek to interpret Job's suffering as a consequence of his sinfulness). Indeed, by making *ressentiment* theological, that is, by linking it to human sin, the Church claims the right to condemn and the authority to be obeyed. Thus Nietzsche suggests, 'By allowing God to judge they themselves judge; by glorifying God they glorify themselves.'[6] Elsewhere he comments, 'Supreme Law: "God forgives him who repents" – in plain language: who submits to the priests'.[7]

The priest saves his flock from the destructive effects of a theology impregnated with violence and revenge by redirecting its energy back upon the individual believer. A society in which the theological imagination has become so shaped by the desire for vengeance is dangerously unstable. The job of the priest is to translate violence directed towards another into violence directed towards oneself. This is the reason why Christianity came to be so important to the political management of society. It is here, Nietzsche believes, that we see the psychological origins of guilt and of Christian notions of original sin. Christianity, Nietzsche concludes, leads inevitably to self-hatred, a masochism he sees exemplified fully in the exultation of a broken and tortured body as the proper object of worship. It is thus that he understands his attack upon Christianity as something liberating, and the 'death of God' as an occasion for celebration. Nietzsche's own prescription for health and for overcoming *ressentiment* lies with the *Übermensch*. This most famous of Nietzsche's characters, depicting perfect human (physical as well as 'spiritual') strength is not an image of some proto-fascist, as is often read, but of one who can break this cycle of revengefulness; of one who is able to rise above the instinct for revenge through a triumphant show of strength. Only by being strong can one resist the temptations of *ressentiment*. Only by rejecting any sense of oneself as victim can one construct a morality free from the pathological and resentful imagination of the slave. And the way to do that is to reject Christianity root and branch. The *Übermensch* is, for Nietzsche, an image of redeemed humanity.

Is Nietzsche right? Certainly the extent to which the Christian tradition has been bound up with violence provides a prima facie case in his favour. Bullying does breed bullies. Suffering can dehumanise as well as edify. And any system of religious belief which presents itself through stories of great suffering must recognise these dangers. Violence has an infectious quality about it, an ability to perpetuate itself even through institutions and systems of thought that are intended to over-come it. Nietzsche's claim is that those who, in the name of Christ, come to heal may end up spreading the infection even deeper into the wound. To quote from the prophet Amos: 'But you have turned justice into poison and the fruit of righteousness into bitterness' (Amos 6:12 NIV).

3. Mimetic Desire and the Purpose of Sacrifice

Now we come to Girard. In a sense, his account is not dissimilar to that of Nietzsche, but, as we shall see, it ends not with a condemnation but with a recommendation of Christianity. Girard's argument begins with an analysis of the role of violence in the construction of human culture in general, and religious culture in particular. The key to understanding the extent of violence within human culture is, for Girard, to be found in understanding the way we learn. Human beings are fundamentally social beings and learn by imitating others. Patterns of behaviour are developed, in the first instance, by copying those around us. If I want to have a bath in the evening I can be quite sure that, all of a sudden, my three-year-old daughter will want one too. If one child wants to play with the toy farm, so will the other. And it is not simply that we learn to copy others' actions, for the whole process of 'mimetic desire' is responsible for the construction of our very sense of self and identity. I am not born with a ready-made identity, I become who I am in a continual process of relating to others. This process involves both attraction and repulsion, both poles of which exist under the logic of mimetic desire. On the one hand I copy those whom I am attracted to. And yet also, in order to make space for a 'me' (a 'me' that is original and authentic) I also deny the extent to which my desires are mediated through the desires of another. Carving out my own place in the world, asserting my own unique individuality, means, very often, a rejection of precisely those who have influenced me most. We might call this adolescence.

For Girard, the whole process of mimetic learning tends towards violence. My younger daughter, learning the desire to play with the farm from my eldest, starts to battle with her sister over the farm. Some things, of course, can be shared. Others cannot. James Alison gives the example of a young lad who admires another – his dress sense, his record collection and so on. These things can be shared, though even here certain resentments may begin. For one may resent being copied and the other may resent the suggestion that he is indeed copying his friend (and the jibes that imply he ought to get 'a life of his own' – to use a rather telling phrase). In both cases the resentment builds through a sense that one's individuality is being threatened. However, if 'mimetic desire' leads one to fancy the other's girlfriend, then here is something, which (I take it) cannot be shared successfully. And trouble is clearly in store. The consequence of learnt desire is that we become rivals chasing the same ends. This rivalry, Girard believes, always ends in tears. Competition for the same learnt desires brings us inevitably into conflict with others and so results in violence. I have given rather homespun examples of this. But clearly the whole idea that learnt desire leads to various forms of rivalry can be given a far more sinister inflection. Making space for a unique me involves the attempt to 'murder' those through whom my desire has been mediated. If not literally, then at least metaphorically; as if what we require is a sort of ontological *Lebensraum* which must occupy the space of others and annihilate them in order to flourish.

Now it may be that you question Girard's understanding of the link between mimesis and violence. I won't defend it any further than I already have. However, Girard's argument does not, I think, stand or fall on the success of his account of mimetic desire. The important element, as far as Christianity is concerned, is how the argument proceeds. The next move in Girard's account focuses on how a society manages its own proclivity for violent rivalry. For violence, once unleashed, is almost impossible to stop. If I punch you, you will probably feel like punching me back. Violence breeds violence. It is 'an interminable, infinitely repetitive process'. And Nietzsche's work can be seen as a revelation of the subtle and underground ways in which violence reproduces itself. But there are, of course, more obvious examples. Think of what is happening, as I write, in Kosovo. Not only do we have Serb and ethnic Albanian locked in a (seemingly) unending cycle of tit-for-tat violence, but even the NATO response to the violence of Slobodan Milosovic is yet more violence.[8] For many, the sense that we need to return violence with violence is unshakeable. Even those unhappy with this state of affairs are at a loss to give a full account of a better way. As Girard writes:

> There is no universal rule for quelling violence, no principle of guaranteed effectiveness. At times all the remedies, harsh as well as gentle, seem efficacious: at other times, every measure seems to heighten the fever it is trying to abate. Inevitably the moment comes when violence can only be countered by more violence. Whether we fail or succeed in our effort to subdue it, the real victor is always violence itself. . . . Violence is like a raging fire that feeds off the very objects intended to smother its flames.

This last sentence reminds us of Nietzsche's account of what happens with Christianity.

How then can a society stop itself from falling apart, how can it contain the violence that continually wells up within it? What is needed is some sort of 'safe detonation' of the violent impulse. Instead of punching me back you may go down to the gym and punch a punch-bag, thereby releasing your aggression. For Girard, sacrifice is precisely that, a 'safe detonation' of the violent impulses which threaten to consume society. Sacrifice is a mechanism by which a society saves itself from the potentially devastating effects of communal violence which are consequent upon mimetic desire. It is an outlet for violence which otherwise would perpetuate itself in a never-ending cycle of reprisals. 'Violence,' Girard claims, 'is not to be denied, but can be diverted onto another object, something it can sink its teeth into'.[9] That something is the sacrificial victim; the one upon whom violence can be vented without unleashing further violence – which would threaten to consume society. Sacrifice is thus a means of avoiding the self-destruction of society. Instead of striking his wife the angry husband kicks the dog – his marriage is (supposedly) thereby protected and his anger assuaged. This is, of course, a horrid example. It is intended to be. For what I want to emphasise is the extent to which the salvation of a society (or marriage) can be premised upon an act of the most terrible savagery.

The relationship between a 'safe-detonation' of communal violence and the activity of scapegoating is at the very heart of Girard's position. Sacrifice is a way of regulating violence. A community threatened by its own violence unleashes that violence upon an innocent and ineffectual other. The feuding parties redirect the animosity they feel towards each other onto one who is powerless to fight back. In this way the feuding parties are 're-conciled' and the social fabric is temporarily restored. Consider the way in which Hitler's scapegoating of the Jews worked as a way of 'bringing society together'. It is deeply shocking to find that Hitler's rhetoric about the Jews frequently relies upon the idea that the annihilation of the Jews would effect some form of communal reconciliation for the German people. This is the sort of 'redemption' offered by scapegoating. And it is surely of significance that the term by which we have come to know the Nazi destruction of the Jewish people, the Holocaust, is also a term that refers to the burnt offering sacrificed to God in the temple. Indeed, it could be argued that in the Holocaust the sacrificial mechanism reaches its most horrific manifestation.

For Girard, the sort of salvation offered by temple sacrifice follows this very same pattern. The victim is slaughtered or ostracised to provide a safe-detonation of communal violence and thus to 'bring society together'. We can now begin to see the way in which Girard seeks to expose the 'sacralisation' of violence. Violence is 'made holy' in the temple. Violence disguised as religion does not recognise itself as violence. By locating the act of scapegoating within the temple, violence is purified of its negative connotations. The carefully regulated rites through which violence is channelled, like the various prohibitions associated with blood and washing, become the means by which a community launders its own violence. And the priest becomes the one who acts out violence on behalf of the community. Those who seek salvation through the activity of the temple cannot, however, see that the temple is a 'sacred' abattoir, a place splattered with blood and a cover for the expression of communal violence. None the less, its priests are simply servants of the mob. And it is this same mob-spirit (the spirit of Dionysus, to use Nietzschean terminology) that will cry out for Jesus' own execution.

It must be said that just as Girard's account of the origins of violence in mimetic rivalry is just one part of the picture, so too his account of the nature of sacrifice fails to register the various purposes and different ways in which sacrifice was conducted in the Hebrew Scriptures. Frances Young in *Sacrifice and the Death of Christ* differentiates between communion-sacrifices, gift-sacrifices, sin-offerings, aversion-sacrifices, and expiatory offerings, all of which have different characteristics and are conducted for different reasons.[10] Girard's paradigm seems to be the sacrifice conducted on the Day of Atonement in Leviticus 16. Even so, Girard is right to bring our attention to the close connection between violence and sacrifice. And having brought this connection into focus we can begin to see the same sort of worries expressed by a number of the pre-exilic prophets. This is rather important. For Girard's thesis, as we shall see, can easily be caricatured as taking the Old Testament to reveal an understanding of religion exclusively built upon the violence of the sacrificial mechanism, and the New Testament as rejecting that model wholesale. This is not Girard's position.

Evidence of the counter-cultural subversion of the sacrificial mechanism is to be found throughout the Hebrew Scriptures. Consider Amos 5:21ff. or Micah 6:6–8 (NIV):

With what shall I come before the Lord
    and bow down before the exalted God?
Shall I come before him with burnt offerings,
    with calves a year old?
Will the Lord be pleased with thousands of rams,
    with ten thousand rivers of oil?
Shall I offer my firstborn for my transgression,
    the fruit of my body for the sin of my soul?
He has showed you, O man, what is good.
    And what does the Lord require of you?
To act justly and to love mercy
    and to walk humbly with your God.

And similarly in Psalm 51:16–17 (NIV):

You do not delight in sacrifice, or I would bring it;
    you do not take pleasure in burnt offerings.
The sacrifices of God are a broken spirit;
    a broken and contrite heart,
    O God, you will not despise.

And perhaps, for Christians most significantly (because it is picked up by Jesus), we find in Hosea 6:6: 'For I desire mercy, not sacrifice, and acknowledgement of God rather than burnt offerings' (NIV).

For Girard, however, the most outspoken opponent of an ecclesiastical establishment that has based itself upon performing rituals of sacrifice is Jesus himself, and it is in the Gospels that the attack upon the sacrificial mechanism is most fully developed. So it is to Girard's account of the theology of Jesus that we must now turn.

4. Jesus *contra* Religion

Thus far we have seen that Girard believes the essence of 'religion' to be the liturgically-cleansed murder of an innocent victim which establishes temporary peace in a community threatened by its own violent rivalries. Girard notes the extent to which murder of one rival by another is often associated with the founding of communities. He points to Romulus and Remus and the foundation of Rome. Likewise, the foundation of the human community, according to Genesis, comes about through the murder of Abel by his rival brother. Unlike Freud, Girard does not see religion as being built upon a one-off murder but, rather, upon the continual process of scapegoating which has to be repeated as mimesis rises to another crescendo of potentially destructive rivalry. The cult of the temple continually formats and reformats this violent urge as it struggles to unite society with the blood of the innocent victim.

The other feature of the way the temple works to provide a safe, though none the less bloody, redirection of violence is that it must veil its cultural purpose both to itself and others. It cannot see itself as providing a service for the management or reconciliation of society but rather must believe in the inherent guilt of the victim whose sacrifice is required. Why? Because once the truth of what is happening is exposed the manifest injustice of the mechanism is laid bare. Indeed it is possible to read a number of theological arguments rehearsed in the Bible as ways of fending off the realisation that the victim might be innocent. In the book of Job we can see the assumption being made by Eliphaz and his friends that because Job suffers he is necessarily guilty and deserves his lot. What is revolutionary about the preaching of Jesus is that, drawing upon the tradition of the 'innocent victim' in the servant songs in Isaiah and in Job, he seeks to expose the workings of temple violence as complicit in masking the innocence of the innocent victim. This is at the very heart of his altercations with the Jewish authorities. In fact, Jesus' attack is not simply directed at the temple per se, for the activity of scapegoating is formative in human culture in general. The link between mimesis and scapegoating is so fundamental that violence is built into 'the world' itself. On this reading, then, Jesus' hostility to the temple is an extension of his hostility to 'the world'.

In the so-called 'Curses against the Scribes and Pharisees', Jesus sets about revealing the degree to which the religious urge is complicit with the violence of scapegoating:

> Therefore I send you prophets and wise men and scribes, some of whom you will kill and crucify, and some you will scourge in your synagogues

and persecute from town to town, that upon you
may come all the righteous blood shed on earth,
from the blood of the innocent Abel to the blood
of Zechariah the son of Barachiah, whom you
murdered between the sanctuary and the altar'.
(Matthew 23:34–5)

Abel and Zechariah are the first and the last to be
murdered in the Old Testament, and so, just as
a-to-z can stand for the whole alphabet, Abel and
Zechariah stand for the long list of innocent victims
murdered in the course of human history – 'all the
righteous blood shed on earth'. Here begins Jesus'
attempt to unpick the web of theological untruth
that has masked the violence of religion. These
innocent victims, precisely because society comes
to be united as a consequence of their ostracism
or murder, are retrospectively accredited with sot-
eriological significance. Society sees itself as being
saved through the blood of the innocent victim
and so the innocent victim, although murdered by
society, is subsequently celebrated as having
brought conflict to an end and invested with an
aura of the sacred. As Gerard Loughlin puts it:
'Thus the death of the victim becomes the site of
the "sacred", the latter being no more than the
salvic violence that produces peace. It is this sense
of the sacred – which is the experience of peace
through collective murder – that gives rise to
religion, when the victim is deified and the peace
brought about by his or her death is maintained

through the ritual re-enactment of the saving murder.'[11] The scribes and Pharisees, therefore, both want to conceal the innocence of the victim and the violence surrounding his or her murder at the same time as celebrating the victim as holy. According to Girard, this is precisely what Jesus is out to expose:

> 'Woe to you! for you build the tombs of the prophets whom your fathers killed. So you are witnesses and consent to the deeds of your fathers; for they killed them, and you build their tombs.' (Luke 11:47–8)

The image of the tomb neatly captures both the celebration of the 'sacred' victim and the conceal-ment of the murdered body which lies within. Therefore:

> 'Woe to you, scribes and Pharisees, hypocrites! for you are like whitewashed tombs, which out-wardly appear beautiful, but within they are full of dead men's bones and all uncleanness.'
> (Matthew 23:27)

The theological revolution spearheaded by the pro-phets, by Hosea, Job and Isaiah in particular, finds its fullest expression in the theology of Jesus. Quoting from Hosea 6:6 Jesus gives us a perfect soundbite to sum up the radical nature of his thinking: 'Go away and learn what this means. I desire mercy and not sacrifice.'

Like the prophets before him, Jesus contrasts

religion grounded in sacrificial practice with a commitment to 'righteousness' or 'mercy' or 'forgiveness of sins'. All of this one might sum up in the following way: Jesus preaches about, and opens up the possibility of, the kingdom of God – a kingdom which is not built upon the violence and vanity of human nature, but initiates a 'new creation'. Matthew 5:38–48, and all the emphasis on forgiving another and not returning violence for violence, is about not being trapped by a mimesis of the violent other. Forgiveness is, on one level, a refusal to imitate the violence of others and thus begins the reconciliation of all humanity offered by the kingdom of God. We will look at what this means in more detail in the final chapter.

5. The Atonement

So far Girard's account of the workings of violence in religion, and of Jesus' hostility to it, seems relatively unproblematic. There may be weaknesses in his account, but Christians from a broad range of backgrounds should find what he has to say interesting and relatively unproblematic. What Girard offers is a way of understanding why Jesus felt so strongly about the temple and its functionaries. Given, however, that Girard's argument is to become more controversial, it is worth pointing out the extent to which even relatively conservative Christian voices are prepared to acknowledge that Girard is on to something. For instance, in a collection of essays published following a symposium on the atonement at St John's College, Nottingham, in the mid 1990s, the then principal and Old Testament scholar, John Goldingay, writes approvingly of Girard's contribution to the theology of sacrifice. (John Goldingay, 'Old Testament Sacrifice and the Death of Christ' in *Atonement Today*, ed. John Goldingay, SPCK 1995, p. 15ff.) What he does not address, however, is the extent to which Girard's theology of sacrifice leads into a broadside against one of the defining features of evangelical theology – the idea of retributive atonement. For many liberals, there is something deeply worrying about the idea that Jesus' death should be understood as a sacrifice made for the sins of the world. What many tend to find problematic is the interpretation of the atonement in which God is willingly prepared to commit a horrendous murder upon his Son as the means by which humanity is redeemed from its own sin. On Girard's account, this understanding of retributive atonement is not only incapable of redeeming humanity, but is precisely that from which salvation is necessary. That is to say, it is precisely the idea that violence (sacrificial violence or any other sort) can be redemptive that Jesus so wholeheartedly rejects. Indeed he was murdered for rejecting it! If the culture of violent retribution is the problem, how can a violent retribution redeem it? In Girard's account, then, a certain type of Christian theology of the cross serves to reinforce and deepen the very thing Jesus himself railed against.

Let me try and briefly sketch how Girard sees the significance of the cross. The world is character-ised by, and founded upon, violence. To put it another way: the world is ruled over by Satan who (as John 8:44 has it) 'was a murderer from the beginning'. Satan is also the originator of deceit: specifically, he deceives humanity as to the extent to which human institutions (including religion itself) fulfil and perpetuate the satanic will-to-murder. To expand John 8:44: 'He was a murderer from the beginning, and has nothing to do with truth because there is no truth in him. When he lies, he speaks according to his own nature, for he is a liar and the father of lies'. Jesus, however, is innocent of worldly violence. His very nature is defined by the love of God which is in no way complicit in the violence of the world. Jesus' message, to love one's enemy, strikes at the very heart of mimetic violence and the ways in which violence perpetuates itself. No longer an eye for an eye, but, rather, forgive even your enemies. For this reason Jesus stands against 'the world' and seeks to expose its violent constitution by speaking the truth about it – to expose the 'things hidden since the foundation of the world'. On one level he does this by his preaching and teaching – a message that is consistent with that of a number of Old Testament prophets who were murdered for seeking to speak up against the violence of the religious establishment. Jesus, likewise, incurs the wrath of the authorities by preaching the same message. But where Jesus differs is that, as God, he is wholly innocent of the world and worldly violence. As he is put to death, his manifest innocence breaks the hold of the great lie that victims deserve their fate. His death reveals the truth about the human capacity for violence. As the crowd bay for Jesus' blood, for the blood of the wholly innocent, the reality of human violence is unequivocally revealed and Satan's lie begins to unravel. The truth begins to dawn. God reveals – as in revelation – the arbitrariness of human violence. Satan is exposed.

All of this has to be understood with reference to issues addressed in previous chapters, notably (a) the idea that the violence of mimetic desire and scapegoating forms the basis of human culture and (b) that culture can only function in this way by denying its own complicity in violence. The crucifixion exposes the truth of (b), exposes, that is, the lie of acceptable redemptive violence, and by doing so begins the collapse of (a). In its place Jesus offers the reformed mimesis of the kingdom of God.

Let us now contrast Girard's account with a theological model of the cross which takes us in an entirely different direction. Arguably the most important text in the development of the satisfaction theory of the atonement is that of Anselm in *Cur Deus Homo*? – or, Why a God-man? Why the incarnation? His argument has built itself so successfully into our theological imagination that it almost sounds as if it were the very gospel itself. It goes something like this: Humanity has sinned against God and through sin has dishonoured God; as it were, insulted him. The consequence of this is either that humanity must suffer eternal death or make some sort of 'satisfaction' to God for the insult against him.

The implication of sinning against God has to be understood in terms of the way Anselm's society understood that a sin against a more important member of society counts as more significant than one against a less important member. If I strike someone of my own social standing an apology might be sufficient to 'compensate' for the offence. If, however, I as a commoner strike a feudal lord I will probably have to pay with my life. Such logic seemed self-evident to Anselm. And if a sin against one's feudal master demands a death in order to restore honour, how much more is required for a sin against God almighty, the ultimate feudal Overlord. Indeed, the magnitude of this sin is such that nothing a human being is capable of offering can come close to balancing the scales of satisfaction. And, so the argument goes, God cannot just forgive human sin, for in this way God would be failing to recognise a difference between good and evil. This would lead to moral disorder and the beauty of God's universe would be compromised. God cannot, as the right-wing rhetoric of Anselm's theological children often put it, be 'soft on crime'. The inevitable consequence of the combination of these theological positions is that human beings are doomed.

The paternity of popular conceptions of penal substitutionary atonement has, in fact, to be understood as that of Anselm mediated by Calvin. Whereas for Anselm, Christ pays off the debt through offering his life freely to God (a perfect offering which restores honour) it is Calvin who believed the only way for Christ to meet the debt was to suffer *punishment* in our stead. Calvin's view is Anselm's account of debt repayment plus the assumptions of rediscovered Roman criminal law that the only appropriate response to law-breaking is punishment. For Anselm, however, we are saved *from* punishment through Christ's satisfaction. These positions are subtly different; none the less both positions are clearly retributive.

This, then, is why a God-man is needed. God, wanting (or demanding?) both satisfaction for the sin, and recognising the human impossibility of meeting this demand, sends His Son to earth to pay the required compensation. As we often sing at Easter: 'there was no other good enough to pay the price of sin'. Transposed by Calvin, this becomes: Christ makes himself a sacrifice for the sins of the world. As he is tortured and murdered human sin is wiped away.

It must be emphasised that my problem with Anselm's account is not so much with the idea of vicarious suffering – of the moral acceptability of one person suffering on behalf of another – but rather with the idea that justice is necessarily retributive, and that the moral order of the universe, as ordained by God, requires an eye for an eye and a tooth for a tooth. As Girard is at pains to point out, it is precisely this logic that perpetuates violence and continues our estrangement from God. And yet it is this very same logic that is built into Anselm's account of the cross. Defenders of retributive atonement frequently employ a good deal of fancy philosophical footwork to conceal the moral inadequacy of this position. Christina Baxter, for instance, argues that Anselm is misread if he is taken to be claiming that God's justice requires retributive *punishment*, rather, she insists, God's concern is with the payment of a *debt* that humanity could not pay. But what difference does this make? Debt-language is, she evidently thinks, less offensive than punishment-language. Those of us who support Jubilee 2000 and their campaign to persuade the rich countries of the world to abolish third-world debt unilaterally might not follow her logic. Jesus speaks of forgiving others their debts in the spirit of the Jubilee. Baxter, however, writes: 'There is no free lunch at the end of the universe even for God.'[12] All atonement theologies of this basic genre assume the necessity for retributive justice. According to Girard, it is this very logic of retribution that serves to perpetuate violence and it is precisely this theological mind set that Jesus is out to eliminate.

This issue, then, is not simply one of academic concern, but raises a whole host of questions about the extent to which the retributive model that is built into Anselm's account has been used to justify the use of violence in the name of justice and Christianity. The theological justifications of capital punishment (hanging, burning, boiling, etc.) in England up to the mid part of this century are a good case in point. Harry Potter, in his study of this period writes, 'The flourishing of the capital code was a relatively late development, however, and was roughly coterminous with the Protestant ascendancy.' Of course, this does not mean that

traditional doctrines of the atonement so character-
istic of Protestant doctrine of the period were
responsible for hanging. None the less, the atonement was at the scene of the crime egging on the
perpetrators. The central importance of the Church
in the practice of hanging

> ... is explained by the fact that hanging was
> an institution which demanded, even craved for,
> religious sanction. The Church by Law Estab-
> lished provided the intellectual and theological
> justification for hanging ... Judicial killing was
> sanctioned by bishops, and its execution presided
> over by chaplains. Had the church denounced it,
> it would have withered and died, as it did quickly
> and without hope of resuscitation in the 1960's.
> Only in the 1950's, long after all other pro-
> gressive religious and secular opinion had ranged
> itself against capital punishment, did the Church
> of England take a firm stand in favour of
> abolition. . . . For at least a hundred years that
> imprimatur preserved and sanctioned the judicial
> taking of life. Then suddenly and totally the sanc-
> tion was withdrawn, and what had been done in
> God's name became unconscionable.[13]

Even when society at large began to turn against
the death penalty, there were many clerics who saw
this as an expression of increasing Godlessness.
'With irreligion,' writes one, comes an 'un-
warranted tenderness' towards criminals. And still
today, in many parts of the world, it is Christians

(for the most part, evangelical Christians) whose voices are raised in support of the death penalty. In America, for instance, the death penalty has more support amongst Christians than it does in the population generally.

Tim Gorringe sums up the tragic irony of this twisting of the Christian message: 'The suffering Christ, an icon of the wickedness of judicial punishment, became the focus of its legality, and for the need for the offender to suffer as he did.'[14] The impact of retributive accounts of atonement was to legitimate a culture of acceptable violence. If Girard is right this legitimation begins way back in the biblical texts and beyond into prehistory. The story ever since has involved the struggle in turns to reveal and to conceal these manifestations of the sacrificial instinct. And the struggle continues today.

6. Truth and Reconciliation

I promised to return to Nietzsche in the light of
Girard. Few Christian thinkers have been prepared
to take Nietzsche on and, consequently, his attack
upon Christianity has largely gone unanswered.[15]
Girard supplies some of the necessary ammunition.
He begins his defence of Christianity by admitting
that Nietzsche is partially correct. Oppression does
not necessarily turn the oppressed into saints. And
even those who seek to practise forgiveness or
those who turn the other cheek, do so from within
the context of a complex amalgam of motives. For
Girard, what Nietzsche is pointing out is the way
in which the instinct for vengeful reciprocity continues to assert itself even when violent retribution
is foresworn. I may respond to your striking me by
turning the other cheek, but in my guts I still want
to punch you back. That instinct may, of course,
have all sorts of morally significant consequences,
and Nietzsche is right to point them out. But even
so, such consequences are surely a price worth
paying for calling a halt to retributive violence.
Girard puts it thus:

> *Ressentiment* is the interiorisation of weakened
> vengeance. . . .He [Nietzsche] sees *ressentiment*
> not merely as the child of Christianity, which it

certainly is, but also as its father, which it certainly is not. *Ressentiment* flourishes in a world where real vengeance (Dionysus) has been weakened. The Bible and the Gospels have diminished the violence of vengeance and turned it to *ressentiment* not because they originate in the latter but because their real target is vengeance in all its forms, and they succeeded in wounding vengeance, not eliminating it. The Gospels are indirectly responsible; we alone are directly responsible. *Ressentiment* is the manner in which the spirit of vengeance survives the impact of Christianity and turns the Gospels to its own use.[16]

Ressentiment is what is left of vengeance once one sets out on the road for peace. Nietzsche is at his best in seeking out and revealing the instinct for vengeance that hides behind the false Christian smile or the pathos of the victim. However, in times of peace and prosperity it is easy to miss the bigger picture and confuse this interiorised weakened vengeance for the real thing. Girard continues:

Nietzsche was less blind to the role of vengeance in human culture than most people of his time, but nevertheless there was blindness in him. He analysed *ressentiment* and all its works with enormous power. He did not see that the evil he was fighting was a relatively minor evil compared to the more violent forms of vengeance. His insight was partly blunted by the deceptive quiet of his post-Christian society. He could afford the luxury of resenting *ressentiment* so much that it appeared a fate worse than real vengeance. Being absent from the scene, real vengeance was never seriously apprehended. Unthinkingly, like so many thinkers of his age and ours, Nietzsche called on Dionysus, begging him to bring back real vengeance as a cure for what seemed to him the worst of all possible fates, *ressentiment*.[17]

We cannot escape the complex and sometimes deeply ambiguous instincts that surround the act of forgiveness. For Nietzsche these ambiguities are the site of the real sins of Christianity. Girard provides a thread which can lead us out of the psychological labyrinth prepared by Nietzsche. He reassures us that it is the resistance to real physical violence that is primary. The idea that the marauding Viking, because he expresses rather than internalises his instinct for vengeful reciprocity, is a more valuable spiritual role model is a fantasy of another age. The horrors of the twentieth century, from those of the Somme to the Nazi death-camps to Pol-Pot and beyond, make Nietzsche's prescription for spiritual health wholly untenable.

None the less, Nietzsche's legacy continues to haunt us. He has problematised Christian motivation and consequently we can easily become overly distrustful of ourselves. The hermeneutics of suspicion won't leave us alone. 'Am I really doing this (forgiving, turning the other cheek, etc.) out of the best of intentions?' we wonder; and however much prayer or introspection we undertake, these questions cannot be finally settled.

The question behind all of this anxiety is, in a sense, a question of who I really am. Am I really the public me, the me who doesn't hit back, the me who speaks words of forgiveness, or am I really the private me, the me who continues to resent and nurture powerful feelings of animosity. Am I a bad person masquerading as a good one? – that, at least, is what Nietzsche might lead us to suspect about ourselves.

However, the idea that the 'real me' is the hidden, inner me is a complex theological and philosophical mistake. It is, for instance, just the sort of thing that Bonhoeffer was out to attack in some of the most powerful sections of *Letters and Papers from Prison*.[18] For Bonhoeffer, the need to inspect the 'inner life' of a subject before one can confirm the goodness of his or her behaviour is like the gutter press and its insatiable desire for revelations about the secret lives of public figures – 'as if you couldn't adequately appreciate a good play till you have seen how the actors behave off stage'. Commenting upon one of Bonhoeffer's poems 'Who am I?' Rowan Williams writes:

> 'The calm and cheerful exterior that Bonhoeffer was aware of presenting to his jailers and fellow prisoners ... is contrasted with the anger and

impotence within, so that the question "Which is the real me?" is raised; but it is raised to be itself exposed to suspicion. Why should the analysis be in terms of a false exterior persona cloaking a 'real' weakness; what if the truth is that the interior self is in flight from the victory already achieved of the visible person? . . . Bonhoeffer's flesh and blood were in the prison at Tegel, offering sanity and comfort to other prisoners: how if at all that indubitable victory (both the imprisonment and his manifest response to it) should be harmonised with his inner fears is essentially an abstract problem posed in an unnatural isolation'[19]

Similarly, Girard allows us to recognise, *contra* Nietzsche, that the victory of forgiveness is real enough – asking how that indubitable victory should be harmonised with our inner fear is an exercise which, however compelling, must not lead us astray. For the most part, *ressentiment* is the residue left over from the defeat of violence.

But what, in fact, does it really mean to speak about the defeat of violence. Girard writes of a reformed mimesis and of forgiveness as not being trapped in repetition of the violent other. It might be theoretically clear that forgiveness can function as the lynchpin in a theology of salvation which is completely different to that premised upon retribution. But what might this mean in practice?

One example springs immediately to mind, that

of the Truth and Reconciliation Commission (TRC) set up in South Africa to investigate and report upon the atrocities committed under apartheid. Certainly the aims and objectives of the TRC were to steer a path between a retributive model (which would undoubtedly have served to perpetuate further violence) and one which simply ignored the past, letting bygones be bygones. There are plenty of examples of both approaches. Though we might think first of the Nuremburg trials, perhaps the most disastrous implementation of retributive justice in modern history is that of the Treaty of Versailles. The extent to which the punitive and retributive model of justice inherent in the Treaty of Versailles created powerful resentments that opened the way for the Nazis has been well explored. South Africa could not afford to rip itself apart in perpetuating violence through retributive justice. Nor, however, could it simply declare a blanket amnesty. This second way of dealing with a country torn apart by bloody internal strife can be seen to be that adopted by the Spanish or in Argentina and Chile with respect to the brutalities of their respective fascist histories.[20] And this certainly looks very much like being 'soft on crime'. The TRC, on the other hand (following, to some extent, the way the former GDR dealt with its Stasi past), seeks neither of these. Reconciliation cannot be premised upon retribution or upon forgetting.

Desmond Tutu, the chairperson of the TRC, in his foreword to the report, writes:

> We have been concerned that many consider
> only one aspect of justice. Certainly, amnesty
> cannot be viewed as justice if we think of justice
> as only retributive and punitive in nature. We
> believe, however, that there is another kind of
> justice – a restorative justice which is concerned
> not so much with punishment as with correcting
> imbalances, restoring broken relationships – with
> healing, harmony and with reconciliation.

Fluffy words from the liberal elite? This, of course, is what those of a retributive disposition often claim. But here, evidently, it is quite different. Restorative justice is being advocated precisely by those who have suffered the beatings and imprisonments of apartheid. *Ubantu*, the recognition of the inter-relatedness of all in society and of the need for communal healing through truth telling, has been a practical and politically realistic way of helping create the new South Africa. For as one reads the report of the TRC one becomes aware of the powerful, difficult but none the less potentially restorative value of truth – 'healing' truth, as the TRC reports it.

A few words on this use of truth are, I think, worthwhile. Typically, the Christian tradition in speaking about truth has been concerned with 'the truth of Christian doctrine' or 'the ultimate truth', understood as a quasi-philosophical idea. Here, however, we have another crucial dimension to truth being brought out: truth-as-honesty. This is, in fact, precisely Nietzsche's concern. And the problem with Christianity, as he sees it, is that it has been insufficiently honest about itself; insufficiently honest about its own motivations, or the complexity of the various motivations that underpin talk of goodness, for example. The demands of honesty are often more strenuous than the demands of searching for the Truth, understood philosophically. Christians often think that to be, as it were, 'in the truth' is to have beliefs about God and the world that are true. In their very different ways, both Nietzsche and the TRC remind us of an order of truth that is different from this, an order of truth that requires courage rather than intelligence, one which engages our capacity for soul searching rather than academic rigour. This, one might say, is the sort of truth the Holy Spirit leads us into.

This attempt to reclaim a sense of truth-as-honesty helps us understand why Christian truth is considered a moral virtue. On one level, there is something odd about the idea that having true opinions about the world is a moral virtue. Does, for instance, my having mistaken beliefs about the way gravity works, or the authorship of the Pentateuch make me morally deficient? Surely not. The dons here in Oxford may well know more of 'the truth about the world' than the rest of us, but that clearly doesn't make them any more virtuous. But there *is*, surely, a great moral virtue in honesty. One might argue that this distinction helps us understand something about Satan. Satan, on one level, knows the truth – of how the world works, even of God's existence. What Satan lacks, however, is sufficient courage for truth-as-honesty. Thus (and here is a strangely Nietzschean reading of Satan), Satan becomes Satan through cowardice, a sort of moral and spiritual cowardice that refuses to face its own reflection. To this extent popular horror films have one thing right: evil hates mirrors. And this is why Girard links the revelation of truth to the defeat of Satan. For the truth is judgement.

I see the TRC as modelling something like the sort of account of redemption that is evident in certain parts of the Bible and which I believe to be morally superior to that assumed by traditional models of the atonement. Its message is this: truth is a precondition of reconciliation; upon that is, the kingdom of God. Inversely, refusal of truth is a denial of salvation. Take, for instance, the sub-mission, or should I say non-submission of Winnie Mandela to the TRC. Mrs Mandela, though she came before the commission, refused the oppor-tunity honestly to face her part in the atrocities committed under apartheid.[21] What can we say to Mrs Mandela? Perhaps this: 'If we say we have no sin we deceive ourselves and the truth is not in us: but if we confess our sins God is faithful and just and will forgive us our sins and cleanse us from all unrighteousness.' Which is to say, Mrs Mandela, in refusing the opportunity to face the truth, and in refusing the judgement of truth, places herself outside the kingdom of God.

Confession is no easy option. Indeed, there is a way of seeing the rather clear-cut approach of retributive justice as a good deal softer than the approach employed by the TRC. Retributive logic tends to divide us up very simplistically into goodies and baddies; those who deserve punishment and those who don't. This can be clearly seen in the Treaty of Versailles. The truth, however, reveals complex layers of complicity that cannot be sought out by the blunt instrument of retributive justice. What, for instance, of the complicity of the person who stood by and did nothing? What of the complicity of those companies which invested money in South Africa and helped to sustain the apartheid governments? And what of my complicity in buying South African products? Retributive justice ignores the complicity of millions by focusing upon the clear-cut villains. And in punishing them, our blushes are spared. The dualism of innocence and guilt seems a soft abstraction compared to the rigorous demands of a long look in the mirror.

Of course, there are criticisms to be made of this use of 'truth'. From a Foucauldian perspective, suspicions are raised that the language of truth and reconciliation makes an attempt to impose a particular authority or interpretation (of the ANC over Inkatha, for instance). The TRC can thus be seen as legitimating the hermeneutics of victor's justice as it were. And there are, of course, many other criticisms too: that a great many crimes went unexamined and many perpetrators were not brought to book. No doubt there is more work for honesty to do. And there always will be. Tutu writes: "A Dutch visitor to the Commission observed that the Truth and Reconciliation Commission must fail. Its task is simply too demanding. Yet, she argued, "even as it fails, it has already succeeded beyond any rational expectations."" Could we ask any more of the Church itself? Perhaps Girard's soteriology of forgiveness, like the perfectionism of the Sermon on the Mount, presents us with challenges we will always fail. Perhaps also it is impossible and unrealistic to ask a fallen world to live by the values of the kingdom of God. The Church must be mad enough to try. And sane enough to keep on trying.

Notes

1. Quentin Tarantino, Pulp Fiction, Faber and Faber, 1994, p.33
2. See Erich Zenger's excellent *A God of Vengeance? Understanding the Psalms of Divine Wrath* (Louisville, Westminster, John Knox, 1994).
3. Alfred Dymond, *The Law on its Trial* (London, 1865), pp. 287ff.
4. Friedrich Nietzsche, *On the Genealogy of Morals* (Cambridge, Cambridge University Press, 1994), I:15.
5. ibid., II.16.
6. Friedrich Nietzsche, *The Anti-Christ* (Harmondsworth, Penguin, 1986), p. 158.
7. ibid., p. 139.
8. The Church has also had its part to play in the history of bloodshed that has affected this part of the world. At about the same time that the popes were sending crusades to crush the Albigensians in Southern France, so they were sending soldiers to destroy the Bogomils in Bosnia-Herce-govina. Pope John XXII writes to Stephen, the Ban of Bosnia in 1325: 'Knowing thou art a faithful son of the Church, we therefore charge thee to exterminate the her-etics of thy domain . . .their speech crawleth like a crab and they creep in with humility, but in secret they kill.' Richard West, *Tito and the rise and fall of Yugoslavia* (London, Sinclair-Stevenson, 1994), p. 9. Murder has followed for many centuries.
9. René Girard, *Violence and the Sacred*, tr. Gregory (Baltimore, Johns Hopkins University Press, 1977), p. 4.
10. Frances Young, *Sacrifice and the Death of Christ* (London, SCM, 1975), pp. 21ff.
11. Gerard Loughlin in 'Introduction' to *The Postmodern God: A Theological Reader*, ed. Graham Ward (Oxford, Blackwell, 1997), p. 99.

12. Christina Baxter, 'The Cursed Beloved: A Reconsideration of Penal Substitution' in *Atonement Today*, ed. Goldingay (London, SPCK, 1995), p. 72.

13. Harry Potter, *Hanging in Judgment: Religion and the Death Penalty in England from the Bloody Code to Abolition* (London, SCM, 1993), Introduction.

14. Timothy Gorringe, *God's Just Vengeance* (Cambridge, Cambridge University Press, 1996), p. 23.

15. See Giles Fraser, *Holy Nietzsche: Experiments in Redemption*, Ph.D. thesis, 1999, University of Lancaster.

16. René Girard, 'Nietzsche versus the Crucified' in *The Girard Reader* (New York, Crossroad Herder, 1996), p. 252.

17. ibid., pp. 252–3.

18. Dietrich Bonhoeffer, *Letters and Papers from Prison* (SCM, 1953).

19. Rowan Williams 'The Suspicion of Suspicion: Wittgenstein and Bonhoeffer' in *The Grammar of the Heart: New Essays in Moral Philosophy and Theology*, ed. Bell (Harper and Row, 1988).

20. 'Forgetting the recent past in post-war Spain was both enforced by authority and employed as personal and collective strategies of survival. A kind of tacit agreement to forget was entered into. This "pact of oblivion", as it was known in political circles, became an important condition of the process of the peaceful transition to democracy in the 1970s and 1980s' Michael Richards, A Time of Silence: Civil War and the Culture of Repression in Franco's Spain, 1936–45 (Cambridge, Cambridge University Press, 1998, pp. 11–12).

21. The case of Mrs Mandela and the activity of her 'football team' is a good illustration of the ways in which retributive 'justice' can easily perpetuate violence. It does seem clear that, on the instructions of Mrs Mandela, a young boy called Stompie Seipei was abducted from the sanctuary of a local manse and murdered under suspicion of being a spy. One of the murderers subsequently confessed: 'I slaughtered him. I slaughtered him like a goat. We made him lay on his back and I put garden shears through his neck.' Bishop Peter Storey, leader of the Methodist Church in Johannesburg at the time, commented: 'The primary cancer may be, as was,

and always will be, the apartheid oppression, but secondary infections have touched many of apartheid's opponents and eroded their knowledge of good and evil. One of the tragedies of life, sir, is it is possible to become like that which we hate most, and I have a feeling that this drama is an example of that.' There is an obvious Girardian reading of this passage in terms of mimesis ('it is possible to become like that which we hate most') and sacrifice ('I slaughtered him like a goat').